The Death of Galahad

Domenico Iannaco

The Death of Galahad

a poem
written in English thought of as
the common language of Europe.

The Death of Galahad
published in the United Kingdom in 2016
by Leslie Bell trading as Mica Press
47 Belle Vue Road, Wivenhoe, Colchester, Essex CO7 9LD

www.micapress.co.uk | info@micapress.co.uk
ISBN 978-1-869848-06-4

Copyright © Domenico Iannaco, 2016

The right of Domenico Iannaco to be identified as the author of this work has been asserted by him in accordance with the Copyright, Designs and Patents Act of 1988.
All rights reserved.

No part of this book shall be reproduced or transmitted in any form or by any means, electronic or mechanical, including photocopying, recording, or by any information retrieval system without written permission of the publisher.

I.   The ruin of Europe

i

Nobody was in Time in the beginning,
Nothing existed but
Light and darkness,
Dreams over the Void,
Nothing more - no burning core.
What is the first word of love?
Love, I said that it's not our tale...
But still light is,
With its hues it shaped storms
Of rabid thoughts and was poured
In every mouth but our words
Are full of frauds and rob
The meaning which was pure,
A painted one, when the lines cross
The colours which remind of that
Time when there was hope
that something could have been born.

Another winter
Swollen with unusual heat
Passed away and I spent my energy
Among these firs.
I felt the blow
Winter gave and I thought:
"The cry of the land is what reminds us that
The mind of Europe
Has been defiled now because it was
Not much more than Western steam,
I sweat because I am the worst
Of a generation of bastards who conquered the land"
And I weep the condition of this Self.
Be strong my heart,
Maybe you have to tell

The same truth
In your words
And new gems are hoarded there.
The mockery
Speaks
About the simplicity of the way
But now I hear
What was mine only.
The new philosophers have betrayed us
And my realm is chaos.
The body of destruction is among us,
It is not a question of fire but
Confusion
Which hisses in different languages
And it is rich like a blanket of mud,
Left to root and take disgusting forms,
The sense of direction is lost.
What was the top is now at the bottom
Of the clay coloured pond.
The water is stale and doesn't stream,
Like brackish secretion of a carcass
Hanging from the ass.
Dead bream hint that the stink is
The goal of life drying on
Shales of lore and gore...
Can you imagine what has no shape?

When you lose the landmark,
The shortcut is sad.
Mull over the lavishness
That is everywhere.
You'll be disgusted because you are the heir.
I mean that
The world is rich
In feeling, sensations, everywhere,
But you are there
With yourself.

They lost their new way
Must everything come back to Christ?
The pursuit of Happiness is a fraud
Because you are more than an urge to pleasure
Spent in haste.
Men and animals
Are promiscuous here.
I can tell you who it was kept me alive.
If Christ is blurred
I can only say that I want to build
On the rock, on him and so
The key that is conscience
Will be thrown away.
An ancient knight, Galahad,
Will spring from my rage.
His mother was a fairy...
My feminine side...
A broth of thoughts
Is Galahad, is my cloudy mind.
The Conscience is Christian and
What I mean is that the body outgrew the mind
And crossed the line
Adjoining Hell.
What was Roman is in me.
But I have many voices.
My responsibility will arise.

ii

The dark splashes and moves ashore
Like a wave leaving
Stains,
Letting you think that
This tsunami screams.
It's a way
Of saying farewell.

You believe in moving forward
And breaking the fence of what
A human mind was and
It's rich, the taste
Which ticks among your teeth
You suck the melted juice
Then bite what you may not eat.
History? The drama of Adam and Eve?
The birth of Everyman is a real story
Because he thought he had come
After the man
And he was
A dream of gross supremacy.
He killed the ancient animal bond.
He was bald.
He stinks like a corpse,
Which is left to worms in copses
From which the smell is pregnant
Of everlasting drops of anger,
Brewed for the denouement and
Ready to be unleashed like a pack
Of famished dogs,
His spirit is not recollected in words.
So he understood that he could forge
His drug
And move the world
Like an element
Behaving like a fool
Happy in Hell, who wants
To stamp its track in the land
And dictate his idea of future.
"Galahad was with the relics
Of a past which was holy
But finally he rose.
A field of forces is moving
Its banner against me.
He recollected the old myth.

He said, 'I'll re-write the legend'.
But I called the scrap yard
Around me Paradise. I conquered what's elusive
Inside us. I have many voices.
I am a beehive.
The chaos itself works for me,
It heaved
The lid of mist which has hidden the sky.
I am everywhere.
The fellow is handsome
Like the photo of a princess,
Like the opening of blue eyes
After a long sleep.
I must kill him,
This strange kind of bird".
"I am Galahad.
When my father knew my mother
He was drunk. For my mother
It was a duty.
In return she had to live my life.
Hence I am a tool with different uses.
A funny way to age well
Or a saint sent to generate in the world,
This call was my real fall!
Hence, I am here
And I know there's a God.
He has overwhelmed me
But Predestination spells
My mood.
My God, I don't know if you are good.
If in this life there's only soup
I must sip,
I'll fight against everything.
I saw what rational mind is,
A mere technique, born
To solve and win,
Untying the knots of

hidden sorrow
Which should have hugged me.
And the fall of conscience is celebrated
Into the wild.

Frances,
Give me the strength
To jettison what I bear and to
Catch fire
Outside.... I want to be a sign...
Despite being frail...
A human body, the language
It suckled, Me. This is me.
You were before.
Is there Freedom beyond these vapid seasons?
I simply don't have a reason,
Because the undertow of a new world
Can get you drunk,
Burn common sense,
And you'll cradle Fay, her arms around you.
Your barbaric song can destroy
The civilisation to which you belong...
I hate this world, it's a kind of toy, but
I must assume I am not so strong
The forbidden knowledge
Yields a new future. Perhaps
A Romanian prostitute to screw.
Spring is a season of war,
I would offer the blood of a nation to
Chew it another time.
It will be lit again
What can harm
The myth
I have been?
We have worshipped our seed
And lowered what was bright.
We celebrate penis and pain.

So the fourth horseman, me,
Will come
As sad as
The resistance of life
Which doesn't want to forget...

Every poet dreams
About what will come
After this shebang!
I want my Time
To be in a deeper communion
With what is really mine,
And show off a power
Which was lost,
For the last time
A power
Which now is a ghost,
Can Frances smile?
Moment, let me see the end,
When my Europe will be melted
In a glass that will blow off
Like the body of Galahad.
I am not ready.
I want to see the vanity outside...
Progress is in my veins
It's time to judge my land.
Now is the time
Which was meant for me.
Poetry will take its revenge
Because it belongs to the dead.
If Apocalypse must be
Let me destroy my rationality.
I am only a drive,
A funny condition
But as Hamlet would say
An idiot tells the truth.
My sarcasm is part of my faith.

I can tell
I hate what I touch,
But I really drank my time.
I was intoxicated
By its poison
And the hues of the palette
A man can use
have the scent of blood
In this stuffed oubliette.

Because I felt raped
By what was around.
I am a man. I must be strong.
Why can't I melt away and be
Eaten by the rocks?
I want to percolate like the rain,
But this fire rises
And the wind is like steam
In my lungs
I feel horny and hot,
And I am simply so".

I, Galahad

It was a dark age for
mankind. Hence
Frances, nodding to
the purple Sunrise,
simply smiled.
I have lost my angel,
Life is too long
And I breed in abstract words,
Changing particles of evil
To fissile action, shale
worth no comment.
Why did I endure this moment,
Why am I aware of this Momentum?

I cannot change life
and I outlived my dream.
The Zephyr knew its nature
And became a hurricane, a wind stream.
"The secret hidden among the shells,...
Was written in the prophetic
Book about the grey knight of King Arthur.
Its rhyme is as imperfect
As the rain that rinses the soul,
Leaving open knots of miry skin,
sins of the sharp drops.
Soul, mauled by the flint,
Christened by the wind.
An excess of Self nailed
The shield of fear and consciousness
Into the white wall of nonsense,
Because Hell is molten here and spreads
Among the rooms of your Self.

I wanted to force Providence
Into giving vent to spread my scent...
Wallpaper, waste paper bin,
Are believed to have received the trash
Of my youth, the cash of
My imperfection without
A female love, but I shaped her ghost
And her face was not so human
Among flaxen curls, then this rape which
Is the poisoned cup of being between
Good and evil maybe...

Yes, I don't pose,
I bought the carnal limits
Of what is real, because
Under that sign, the flag of
"Ideal", I confused the in-seeing voice,
Only to move forward

And watch the counterpoint
Of my devilish choices.
Mystery is a continent
I pretend to ignore.
My angelic hands are sore,
But I can't pretend and I act inspired by
The lonely spires of that purity which can't be,
I mean the scope of this hypocrisy.
A love-story waits, the romance seems
To be set like a crisis, to be mean.
You'll understand
Why I collapse. Carbon is in my gut.
I played with my cattle
But now it's time I recollected:
I had a name, I had a body, which grew
Where the Madonna's lily was burnt,
And so
The Apocalypse is as common
As the daily daisy
On the silent hilltop
Of Silbury Hill,
When the wind is still...
I had a body, yes,
A copy of my wasted age
But I can't condemn this life.
I am here for the quest
Although
What you call Reason,
Future and sex are not much more than a mess!
Despite the impurity and the rest...
I missed the fear of the second death,
The idea of fire which in the end
Would have imposed a shred of Justice
On this subconscious pond,
Where blades of grass as dark as
Shadows which stalk
Envelop the breath of my heart.

My pale blonde wants me to have
A reaction, but this water scolded me,
I don't know what a real action is.
There's a flux of raped sensations...
Yes... I was a man, I was Galahad
I can only draw this spiral,
Then recoil,
Far from me is
The sphere of the Grail.

A cross takes on the features
Of my Time while
The troops of Doom soon pull out
Of the last boundary of Europe.
It could be
My knights,
The sickness is in the blood!
A new stock of virus was born and a thought
Became your pretty doll.
Close ranks! Close ranks!
Mankind cannot win this fight.
"Mates, you know I have different voices and
speak a language forged in the South.
You implore me
To lead you where the land is broken, its
Thin crust rusts...
What was the backbone of Europe?
The silicon has won, but we fight,
And against who, against what ?
First, I go like a memory,
We mate like pigs,
This is more than a hint.

 I have to collect your debts
That must be paid now. My mother
Knows my heresy. My French name.
You don't know Frances.

You don't know me.
You don't know the torment of the past.

II.   Something about the Grail

"I have a body and so I am,
Clothes and a beret,
Rows of plants and parched thoughts,
Overwhelming calm desires and
A deluge because my soul is
My temptation, it is liquid, it is
Ravenous pride.
And to show I can do what you can't,
I want to possess,
Comprehension and sex,
Every creature and then destroy its real, shaken substance,
Its mean shape.
The shape is a Roman concept.
By destroying myself,
Cherishing my rage,
I can really say "I am",
Rambling like the main
In billows full of stains.

In your town,
Running with the wind,
Accept
That the world
Is still.
But we live like gleams,
Traces that are man.
Despite
The seraph I am,
I ate my body of man,
Because I really feel
This sadism of possession

And so I rule a kind of Empire
Which is the gleam
Of my mind, the slush of my desires,
And they, the children of Tragedy,
Dance the macabre dance.
They know that a knight waits for his eventful fate,
There is a battle in me, the cause of my mourning.
Doom is more than a word that dawns
Like a cloud in the sky reminding the ooziness of
The ink dense like a tissue of jellyfish.
I am the fetid legion, I am fragmented like
My time, which is empty and real.
I lean over to grasp the Grail which
Can cast a shadow on this impure past".

There, the fairy needles
The purity, the unblemished one.
And tongues of rock are sweet in these days
When the gust of wind is tasty
Because you were born here, next to
The Mother's sick lips and the pieces,
The carnal slops which stare at the
Colour of the wind
That you can touch and feel,
The wind which says,
"This is the time of the Grail".
Every perimeter is signed by sights and measures
And meters are mean means. I mean
That my country fell. My identity was felled.
This is felony but the screams last like a mark,
A brand of abstract ideas in human flesh.
Strange desires, lusts, clash
And my slash is for the architecture
Of the mind, silly queen and it has a structure
That is not stale.
But there's an ancient Dragon,
A real snake

Which creeps over you
To caress your organ
Making you endure
Your impotent hatred against yourself.

And so he feels the bleeding of the forces,
He would be ready for his fate
In this sickness which sets the ground,
In a perpetual strain
Without an ending or an aim,
Whose voice is a reminder
You keep inside.

"I stray because the strain
Doesn't restrain
The wellings of the night."

You can't know what happened
To him who forestalled me.
The rear has been destroyed
Here in this volleyed trench
I pondered the remains of The Human
What felt like the weight of fifty stones
And the impact force
Of this inferno
Is a platitude.
The neutral scream will stab and chisel the ribs.
Give me your eyes!
They really enlighten
A mind. Nothing more...
They echoed fresh sensations
But now I am naked amidst
The sawdust of time.
In this giddy day the future won't
Comply with our desires.

III.   To protest

I struggled to love because
The terrible lid of thoughts
Was above me
And I kept boiling,
Spitting youth and
Carnival sex,
Thinking that
I would have been a match for
The girl who danced like a ghost
Because I loved that hint of death.
She was hectic like a whirlwind
Tireless like a machine.
I can't stand a flavour
When it's too strong.
I craved a beauty
I could have tamed
Because my real self is not much more
Than spleen. Blood
And skin chiselled to be a youth
So perfect
It could scare me and bring me to the verge of madness,
I could sacrifice to the jarring Void
The jerky years of my very life.
Why can't I age
And be a spirit which is a thing?
I don't want to go where I like.
I want to obey usage
As you do.
My freedom is everywhere.
Why can't I be like you
And love what's not worth my mood?

IV.   By becoming a knight, by becoming pure

The king cried out
And wept his eyes out to warn them against
A demon who was beautiful in a time
When harmony was the purity of the parts but now:
A woman's body destroyed
The toy of God. She had
Eyes as green as the drops
Of rain, or a spring
Which surfaces from Inferno
And she tinges the lea with her hair, but now
It's too cold,
His hysteria writhes,
And he can only whine for
The ruins of ideas and will,
Which thaw
Under the hot storm.
An inflation of the cavity,
This man is Woman's body.
Maybe his stars ignored his sanctity.
Maybe it's only human to feel the Spring.
He had a soul, a time, and
He sold it for the playgrounds
Where presences play and run,
Only to see the last garish limit
Where his garrison stood like a cloud of midges.
We ran out of ghosts and he felt mocked
When he saw in his life a pattern of
Anger against the caresses of life.
Is he pure? He is
A son of Winter,
Who can't act. But his brain burns. He wanted
To be freed from every mother,
From every bloody cord
Which is the token of the folk
To whom he belongs.

As free as the X-rays, the spectre of everything.
Galahad abandoned his fragments,
The first layer and its sediments.
"My visions sleep because
I resemble them, and affection,
I feel, is dirty as hell.
Please, buy human flesh.
They want it and call it mark, market, muck."
He is learning, he is improving,
So he'll be able to speak
Like a solicitor
In a court.
He has been ushered to the bath,
"I'll turn your soul into dust".
The oval is clean
In the visions, in the sin.
Let there be light near Newgrange.
He has just become a knight.
No matter the blood, the brains he spilled
To be pedestalled
And then pinned...

The fairy intervened:
It's sweet to suck the milk...
I was weaned off it.
Shape told me:
"You must defend the wall.
Don't think about
What you can suffer from.
The evil is far from you and it came
From another land
And when the young sunrise
Squirts its humour
You will see the dust playing with the plaits of the sun,
In the cathedral where you got your name.
I'll let you drop your head
On my bosomy chest.

Maybe this was an act of love
And Scientists witnessed in the receding light
The flowering of new stars which
Opened the eyes like malleable burning leaves,
Booming with heat and slime of pearls
Pregnant with the tools of life
Which was percolating in waves
Which took gravitational
Magnitude to deliver a cosmos
That now is old,
Maybe after infinite throes, and resounds
In their ears like hiss of wolves wrapped
In wood and ice... the light launches
A new challenge to the void
And pits against the mere nonentity
The browny pulp of human flesh:
The flag of Galahad.
You are not gentle creatures and sail
Constantly to the sunset
Where the limit
Is waiting at the gate and
A man tried with a spade,
Made of the subtlest words
He can conceive,
To uproot the will
To come back to the Void,
The love for the tearing apart of the hinges
To feel again the pulp in human flesh
The common pit is in background where
Your frame and eyes will get rusty
Like weapons of another age.
The presence of the real abyss,
The bliss of sadistic possession of mere life and time
Which shies away from the mushy heart
This Planet Earth had,
Maybe it was strewn with its identical filth
And that is simply a consequence of

Broken experiences, greasy lies
Which fill up the internal landfill
of every human being.
Men, full with lust and false ideas,
Want to penetrate the nature of our genes,
to claim as theirs the secret of our red clay.
I am a creature, they think they are not.
They do not to cure the wounds
Every time brings. They pollute the brain
and scatter drugs..
I am as guilty as them but not so confused
That I would say that madness is truth".

"You are the Death?
"No, my name is Frances. I am only the light."

Our nature is fickle,
And it's stupid to refuse help
But if you want to fight with me,
You must march and not know
That we are going to Rome.
In this book is written
The story of Galahad,
The first man who came
To fight the boundless chaos. It reads:

V.   **Lent**

i

He wished he had seen
The day of destruction,
Craved maybe because that day
Would have meant the end of pain.
And pain cut him off
And made him dry like the bark

From which he barks,
Because in this new world
Of glass and plastic he glanced at
The face of Lord Winter,
The fourth knight
Who is gutting the uterus of the Night.
And he was horrified because he saw
The collapse of what he stood up for.
He has just blessed the knot
Of a new knowledge,
Stoned birds, why are you singing?
Where is the snow?
"Why I can't win over Death?
If I think and milk the stars
Why do I have to meet this task
Which makes me deal with the abortion
And move beyond the slash
That would have been a baby?
She was green like the gleam
Of the Moon.
Don't cry for me
You'll be swept away
I, Galahad, cry for
The daughters of the Thames,
Where the rain oiled the faces
Of tourists and a river
Sparkled like a joke of Carnival.
This age, when the Mothers sleep...
I can't let loose my anger.
I am not strong enough to slay Time."
He sold his charity
For lust. It was the only way to last.
He wanted a body to buy and purchase,
A female body to overwhelm so as to
Repeat "I am".
A saint is only a name,
A joke of fame.

I saw the coffin and the monks,
Maybe this story is too long.
The flag of Hell: "God is dead".
I added "Now the memory stands dead. He
won't let you, my love,
Repudiate his name and if the land
Denies the creation
His voice will groan inwardly"
My inward-looking voice
Disclosed the secret
That he can't be thought of as a man
But his reflection is here
Like the mark of my Roman blade,
Like the frigidity of a plate.
I was the most perfect
Because I was the last.

ii

Human life, you are harmony
And dissimilarity,
Now your flavour is lost like a
Favour which was given to an
Unworthy guest.
Maybe you rhyme,
But where is your rhythm?
I can't repeat or sing in tune,
It's too different from what my ears can hear
I set my ear on the fur of this lake.
A creature robbed of every voice
Scorns my attempt to understand.

If you are a real nihilist,
Please be consequential, don't speak about man!
Maybe you can foresee the tune,
Because this pond your mind is, talks
To the Moon,

Which reminds us of a frigidity,
Which is the same rigidity of
Landing chaos
The Norns are here
Full of a wisdom, which is a will
To kill, haunting the birds of the wood,
And chasing the cars like a road!

VI.   The lie

i

The first of the Norns spoke.
He was inflated by the wind,
Like a pregnant woman whose womb is
Full of brewed liquid of sheer rage:

"His mother thought he was a cherub
And his female body had to be pure.
The day of his wedding
Came and he kissed his
White bride, Nature itself,
In fits of delirium
Of plumes and breaths.
But Hell must have a door.
I saw her, I saw the bride
Blown away by the wind,
Because Galahad escaped when
He saw her becoming
A flux of immature desires.
The wedding was in hell....
Men think to be wise
But the mystery of the throes
Is only a little sum
Of what they had to pay for,
Becoming old.

Nature is a flux
We can't frame the image
But we won't kiss it
As if it were a flaxen love.
Then, the swan appeared.
But it's hard to be alive
And lull a desire
Without a sure aim.
All his memory has been effaced
And he tries to recollect: but he won't accept
He is stained as a man and so is his soul.
He can't remember because
He is deprived of his knowledge.
"I was my father and my mother,
I gather I'll repeat their sins
Because there's a chain which enchants
And now the world goes asunder
Because the
Past surrenders.
The future is not for me".

Now, he is hers, here, for fighting
And singing about the tale of the fog and, maybe,
Of the swan...
He can't accept the rest.
He can't have chosen the pace.

"Only by forgetting ourselves
Can we have real life.
Guilt looks after me
And has your eyes whose
Shadow darkens my
Crime because I consumed
Your French accent
And I knew that decency stifles me.
I can't let you foal
I hate children and doom

I could have been your husband.
Nothing more...
But the pleasure was not for him.
There are rules in this society.
I hope that this will collapse
But I was confused by my ghosts
And fought to impose on you
A system and a rule.
Your seasons were not mine.
You were too young.
And you were staring at my impatient decline.
Here, I underline your name".

Then, the crow cried:

"If he wants to find the Grail
He has to master this art:
Pass his own seed, deny his myth".

ii

The second of the Norns sang,
Ruffling her golden hair with a
Comb of wood and thinning the
Fire
Of the blue eye, to gain a
Concentration that had to wound:

"You sleep in the water.
You plunged your head into life
And let your soul die.
Mother, sweet in the crystalline grave
Of the waves, lulled by the abstract flux
And the trees which are showering their tears,
Drops of resin flake the resistance
Of the taken insect. Amber is a sombre grave

And they stretch their branches
On the sheet of water,
Velvet for a princess".

I cried
"I can't offer you, mother,
My life and my death.
The reaction of life doesn't
Allow me to die
And it's pathetic to quit here
When the world gives in to a new law
Which has banned the pity of our forefathers.
Only the silence and the chalice,
The poison I didn't drink.
Not the silence of the water,
I want to sip the simplicity of water.
Only the burial among the dead.
Mother, hope is lost.
You gave me a terrible will.
And while in the playground the boys played,
I was burning because
I was not there.
I was not strong as you
And to prove I was a good son
I'll destroy
What you taught me.
This Christian rubbish that clips my wings
Don't you believe that
With their means I would have been
Meaner than them?"

VII.   The side effects of love are too many

i

Passions, not love, move
The spirits of the earth
And toll the dead, forgotten envelopes...
Stained heart, pursued health, dirty sunset
Scathed by the voice of Void.
He had his brain
Washed by the milk
Of a star.
He can guess that
During the obnoxious night
The lights of incest grew up, and
Fed this desert.
We violated
The law of Man and Nature.
This is the meaning,
This is the rain.
Our souls will be cancelled.
Night is a terminus.
The clear aspect is too difficult to be borne,
If the tender night were
The cavity of a mother, he would sleep
And fade away to let
His immature sex
Play with Lucifer, that is ice,
And ice has a real voice,
Not the human noise.
The cell of his thought is
Too small and he sees the night
Like a tragic woman,
Assaulted by the bees.
The cell spills down the dark milk of hell.

"Sometimes the double light shakes.

I can't choose a fate
Such as mine,
But I wanted to have one
To run toward a scene.
No matter how pointless
It is to let
This memory down and to accept
That I have no features,
I am a point,
Maybe a wave, a milky shape.
I want to land
Where I was born. And
So I owned a Grail
When I injured this arm,
And a stain of blood
Could be the oriflamme,
But I drank their milk
And I was poisoned and spat
Soul and debris.
It's not always true
That the flames consume.
It's not necessarily a fire,
Maybe a lit match in the wintry tale
Can remind you of a nest.
It is Winter, maybe.
The army camps near the river.
The air sighs for rest
And among candles of reeds
The soul dreams about peace,
The constellation that is Frances."

ii

Galahad's past is quite dull.
He was quite sentimental,
He waited for her and then
She came...

His first adolescent love
Like Saint Clare with whom
He fell in love then:
She said, "Look for a job,
Your abstractions have gone mouldy
And, I'd like to add, you are not a man,
You are a monster, Greek-style.
Technology is not science
And it is not related to the Word.
The Power outgrow his layer and
Shot like a snake from the shell,
To muster the electric brains united
By a common aim,
To grow with it.
Money will buy your heart and
Forge chains of silicone
To gorge on human frozen pieces."

He married only her eyes

"You can speak about everything
Why is your excess raping me?"

She, she was, maybe, Everyman...
He wanted to partake in her joy
But is it true that his strength must be subdued?
He should have become a father.
If you are not merged with her
How can you understand
The sin?
How can he accept coming
To a compromise
With life?
I tell you.
It's forbidden to die rich.
So, he can only brood
On the dark side,

But I don't know whether
He was unfit to embrace
The promise of peace or
If the guilt was his pride.
He wanted to burden himself
With the secret of manhood
But he went back to his den...
Limbo has his past.
He took it badly and he can't know
If by settling down he could have accepted the law,
Because his scattered soul wanted to live.
But he chose to be
Demure, to be firm,
Against everything.
I am a forgotten Limbo
And every memory mixes in me
Because I do not suffer but I outlast time and spirit
To be a thing that is moved by desires for sins.
I wanted another life, without youth.
A surge of oblivion, to have peace
Close to my sword.

VIII.   Ice

i

Galahad, the nothingness
Of his life,
The effort to build a frame.

"So I was frozen and cried,
I saw the blizzard above
The spaces of London, unleashing
The spirits of the wind,
Which battled for the fenced
Fields, like bats without colours

Or eyes.
You can't taste the dainties of life
In this cold and you call
These wolds, a time of
hosts of carbon, "Hell"...
So God dyes his face and
The swan of a suicide soul
Falls into this prismatic snow, into this
Frozen pagan chest
Which mimics life,
Because the particles
Of the snow crisscross
Your remote cry.
This Winter is
The Oblivion of the drugs, and
Cold desires dressed like crows .
The cosmos itself was a point, was white.
Our city, our electric cells
Don't understand that this inferno
Has more than one sense, it is full of lights,
It is more than white.
So he was frozen and he identified himself
With the movement of the snow,
Because he felt in these clouds...
Yes, he was a worm
He was a knight
But it's hard to deny
That we don't have roots
That we can mulch
And we are used to dying
In a bed to forgive and forget,
In the same crawling wind.

ii

Sucking the bitter marrow is

Another attempt
To die. I wanted to learn to fly,
To melt like warmed clay.
Mine is another ploy.
The debt can't be written off.
The act rapes the fact
That water has given me a chance.
You can laugh, but slobbering words
Is a way to sober up.
Because I run amok
I can't be mocked... Your weakness
Saddened me, Everyman,
Lord of the world where
The pure angels are your foes.
You have tasted the blood of the meek.

iii

There was a man there
Who wanted to teach his friends.
He sat on the chair of Peter
And talked to the wind,
Throwing the tune
Hither and thither.
Everyman spoke, sated after lunch:

"The dreams are migrating East.
So is the economy.
I found myself tied,
Strength was a shape and
From the hole of my throat
I tried to speak
And make fire boil,
Bloody fire,
But you don't know
That blood is wine.

My skin bleeds into a word,
And so language has its birth,
A kind of scream, because the churches
Sink, in this mess. In this mess
I can't experience the soft fire
Which with a point can
Kick out the night,
And cradles your memories
While you sing a lullaby to
A little child, who is my final prey.
If Chaos must be,
I want to be its herald
And promise
Peace to have sex
With all the babes
I get. I am at ease here,
I can endure the jumble
While you deal
With the story of the myth.

The fairy disappears. She told me

'Your blood has to be christened'

A remark but she can't know
Why my veins smell,
I am the world.
I fell in love with a certain girl,
I can't say who it is.
The only sliver I kept with me
Is a wreath of hair,
What then? The future is not for me
Who can only deny.
I subjugated God himself,
Because my despair is frustrated by
Occasions.
As for her, I chopped off her head.

I tried to sit where the layer of flowers near
The Dome
Sleeps
And so mix two colours,
Two different tracks of fossilised life.
I was sitting there and was scared by
The teeth of a cave,
Hidden in a shadow, mine.
However, believe me, I don't know
What the power
Which waits at the gate is
And so, I accepted living
Between the borders
To be fused, then, with Void.

My soul is obese,
Gluten running in my blood,
I could remember my pain
And a clock of consciousness teased
My thought, so I decided to go
Towards the sea, because a bath
Is a new start. I want to prune the coral...
More blood.
And I could find peace
Far from my core, far from free will.
A peace.
I must leave. I am your new Christ.
My body to the infinite
To regenerate in the waves,
The electric twinge of life
Which wouldn't let me forget
How tremendous it was to kiss
The mirrors on which I knelt,
Trying to gather what was happening
To my world, to discover
The face of girl, with my eyes,
Who could have rescued me

From the living, the future,
The clever mind, which is destroying
What I have always been.

My mother was named
Frances I loved my
Reflection... I was her fall,
The cause of her rejection.
I rule. Man is my mule and
The toils of birth belonged to the
human toys,
Which recoil facing their own
Trauma,
Their own past.
Feeble casts...
I incarnated the shape and
The shadow. I am the rules.

If I killed the meek, I had good reasons for it,
This is my pasture!
The western wind blows, do you know?
I am here to set my camp.
I don't hate but I envy your will".

IX.   Hell

i

How can I deny my cowardice?
After a jab of blood, a real rush
I dream about the infinite.
A thought can be not much more than an action.
Then, I settle but I feel rage.
I am Arthur himself,
The mockery of the first myth to save
The world.
But my legions have bagpipes and they scream

And when I wake up
I know that Hell is everywhere.
Hell is common here when you can't emanate
The passion.
If we aligned with the nothing
It's because we lost our philosophy and,
Educated in Maths, I have been trying
To make one up,
Only for you
Because you are good people,
And deserve the quantum leap
To avoid the herald,
That released clusters of bombs on our world.
Plato died and what was pure, beyond
The storm of flesh,
Disappeared. Only the altar is there
Defaced by the new world.
I see in this desert of ice, a church, a stone
Which looms like an ancient heirloom,
Forgotten like a statue erected to exorcise Time
Among frozen tongues of rivers that
Cannot resume their flow.

My soul is that altar and
I don't want sacrifices.
Why can't I plunge in the morass
And give life to the doves?
I dreamt of being so drunk that I'd accept
A vain promise of love,
I am bored with this symbolic code,
I found the ground bore the bones
Of a woman, abused to death.
Her ghost whispered that love has a cost.
The way is long and
I am not so fond of this life.
Beyond this waste land there is
Only an unreal territory where

Pigeons have just turned
Into echoes of a new war.
And he asks: "Why can't I fight the plastic
Surgery and let myself die
Blessed by my slimy father?
The new Middle Ages have begun
And I can only cry, because my mother
Cannot kill me".
Song and ancient rhythm have no meaning
For me. So I pay the bill of my nonsense.
I pleaded and craned forward:
"Remember! The temptation comes...
It is rooted in your presence".
The Past is his flesh.
Flesh of Man, you will be fused
With my dull persistence.
Learn, ancient knight... You can't forget hell...
Become human hell and hope to eat this cell,
You have to face up to the stars.

ii

I don't know if I'll become Everyman.
"My desperate battle against Everyman...
He is greedy and violated
The mystery of my queen
To conquer and to dissolve
The surface of the mirror
Which enchants. This is the Grail,
The spell beyond you
Which says what you are not.
The weight of the height cannot be borne.
When the sunlight shakes,
The wind palsies the lymph
In the arteries of the trees.
My mourning is long and a tunic of petals

Haunts my dreams. The almighty night is here.
The pain is there, it presses the sternum
And I am a voice without sex,
Because you can compare Inferno
Only to the waking of Frances,
When she'll arise,
She'll be devoid of tears.
She won't fall into the pit,
She has no lap
And can't stand
Freedom without creation,
She'll make you fall
Into the ditch
Because you are blind
And lead another
Blind man who thinks
He is a horse.

X.   Saint George

i

They marched amidst a field, dotted
With aborted babies. Biting the bullet
They swallowed the air,
Holding the unpaved side,
Which was made of brooms as
Thick as the hair
Of a puppet you licked
When you were a child.
He thought,
Why didn't they have
The chance I have...
They wizened in silence
Before birth and this is
A privilege because our lineage

Is a chimp and the DNA plays with features
And streaks, that turn a god
Into a stick glued to his puffy rugs, while
The land requires a scarecrow
To get rid of the flock of birds.
But what can be truly essential?
We sold the pride in Death
And are lambs who think about another fall.
"Men, abut here
And cover the butts
Of the first line. Remember,
The voice will roar!".
Fear runs the world. I was Saint George,
Just to face it. The Dragon spreads its tail
And snakes over me, over what is the core
Of what was a man. I stand against disgust
And feel a symbol, like a cross.
The one I saw covered by the faked plastic moss.
But I am fiercer than it
Because I will be annihilated today in my ash,
In what remains of this exploited soul.
Who has seen the cancer in his mitochondria
Can't be scared by the beast of pixels and tin.

Vexilla regis prodeunt inferni.

The dawn comes from West...
Roman army,
Where is your might, now?
They wove the tissues of this land,
Now the calmness,
The sense of a new loss.
The moss has its voice
And cries about the opening
Of the door,
The air force was shot

Down...
When you break every taboo
You must realize that
The flux doesn't depend on you.
The people from the West marched South,
In awe of the fiend which had chosen the battlefield.
So the evil germinates and
The sperm of free will streams
As rain
In the gutter which touches
The inner side of Lady Spring.
It's worse by far than dying to be swayed
By your body and to weep
The freedom I had in my mire...
Now, the sun is black and
Pieces of Men have been strewn
To decorate the field
This is the body of conscience.
The swell of mass taps
Into my same heart...

Be patient, my heart and
Keep your battle array because
There's a link between me and the fallen.
But these are not more men.
They lost the shape,
They are puffed pastry,
Bulimic in a barrack.

Can I eat my mercy?
Blunted is the sword...
I can't scathe the nip
Of this Inferno
Among the ferns.
In this war every war.
The Armageddon will be fought
In a single soul,

But if you tried to fledge your flesh,
You'd be the fiercest beast.
Can I say that the judgment is beyond me?
My friend, you need to understand
That this gum your body is
Will eat the soul and the past.
So I forswore because the storm has won.
You can't be an angel.
I didn't want to be.
But they fell here and
They do not know why.
They pretended it was a sacrifice but
The fate
Must be tasted
To the last drop and
What was discarded here
Can't find quietness
Because if you want
To be the ruin of the previous world,
You must accept that your name is rotten,
And being christened means
That you don't belong to yourself.
Frances gave off her radiance.
She withers now as the decay which follows
Youth, it is a track of compassion
In the tangle of existences, among worms'
Dung.

ii

And so I fought against
That angel who fell.
Red plumes and human flesh
In a vortex of blood and breaths.
My Roman sword, his animal face.
I saw you, my soul, my blonde, who

Flows in the death of sunlight and
Begs the light to kill your Self because
A red word scared my spirits
And in a confusion of sex and water
I let the angel destroy my will.
I am dying and I can't know who
The dragon is, who the man is...
If I had only been a man,
I wouldn't be untying the knot of senses because
My choice is a bible
Of shallow lies. Yes, I fight against myself,
My blonde haired pale-faced girl, and
It was what I gathered from my quest...
Grass and blue desert, but now
I know, by destroying myself, there is hope,
I kill, I live, I survey.
The ripples of thought can't be smooth.
So I remember well,
There's pain everywhere
And I am not free.
I interpreted the role of society
But I didn't want to be a poet.
I am here because I was put here
I wanted only to conquer the world
But then I lost everything
Because the actions absorbed me
And I had to face a routine
Other men,
Obsessions, hysteria
Have imposed on me.

I wanted to be the wind.
But I can't kill.

XI. Wedding day

i

I was wondering, wandering in a wood. Then, I got lost.
So it happened one day
That I knew was my wedding day
I forgot who my bride was,
Covered with a coat of grass and violets,
And fur of pets.
Yes, I kissed her and I learned
What the violence of a hectic dance is.
Young ghosts and female voices
Blessed our union and the elf, her father,
The Russian tycoon,
Was happy because I was a good devil,
But, there could not be a happy ending,
Because I ended up getting drunk,
And I sharpened up a new language,
To infect the sunset of West
And kill the swallow.
They eat
The symbols of this persistence
Which tampers with my existence.
I didn't deflower her.
I bring like a symbol a flower where birds hid.
My bird can't have peace, because
I love all the inexpressive bodies
Singing about the suicide of my pallid doll.
This happened since then.
I stain what I touch and
When I am feeling like
The angel of the Apocalypse,
I desire pity
Of this bird and I want to kiss it.
I regret becoming a legend.

ii

Meanwhile the fallen angels storm out
From the field where knowledge
Can't puzzle out the nature of beauty.
The battle is lost.

iii

The coming of the goddess who
Was wearing violets
As violent as the climax of April
Which whirls on the shores
Where lichen and water
Remember the sex of the slumberer
Who wakes up to grasp
The new rose...
Yes, I arose as powerful as
The surface of the sun, to be
The father who engenders
A new sound.
This is the melting of my senses
When I sense that this Beauty has
An alluring charm which cuts the colours
To give back the pathos of the painting
Where the characters cannot move
And so breath is turned into a naive
Chamber of desires, other sights.
We are all in this immature jail.
Man you must learn
That there's the inhuman logic
There and you can be everything but
Then you will fall into yourself.
Maybe you are a child no more
And the job you have is to continue
What I have never understood.

XII. Temptations

Ashes and dross
Which jar
And are the focus of our stars.
Please, shape the plasm of the blood
And shut up the psalm in this gore,
Which has riven my heart.
I lost and I don't know
What God has in store.
Bloodcurdling is the deterioration
Of Body and Mind,
Their dualism
Choked off in the cream
My real perception is.
They didn't burn the
Hyacinths...
They withered mute and sweet
While waiting for
The slow death of the days
Which warily speak piecemeal.
Everything is
Eroded.
I was a ruin.

Then, the features of the goddess
Shadowing the land!
I die together with my last stave,
Refused while I rave.

The thought of a fluted female
Smile could bring him
To feel the temptations
Of the Divine.
And so he fell in love with Saint Claire.
And he perceived that a virgin
Knight could play with

The halo as well as
With a frilled maid...
But he was a fool,
There is only one world
And, here, men have their slaves.
Shocked by Saint Claire,
He desired to be the landlord
Of the female flesh and Nature...
Now, he knows he is worse
Than King Lear's two daughters,
Because he has paid a girl by using
His spiritual forces
To show a new sadism.
He learnt what
Capitalism really means,
Exploitation even of
Weakness and sex
"I would rather be
The fourth horseman.
In a future, beyond this sky
I will be pure and you'll be mine
In the land I dreamt about.
A storm destroyed my real bride.
I have to apologize
For my mad cat desires..."
"I will be naked and I'll give my bride my
Naked rose...
My red feelings my immodest pride,
The vexillum. But I can't forgive
Myself because
I cannot understand the sense".
Galahad was tempted next to the river and
He would have fallen but
He saw the snakes
Drawing closer in the air
And felt the fear
So he understood

How trivial Frances is
How dangerous this slapstick will be.

"I last. This is my guilt"
If I could die now, I wouldn't be the child of Sin.

XIII. A pledge

The roots of the flower
Are the hair of the buried girl
And cry because the Lent of desires
Has just begun and there are no questions
About this narrow life, about the
Sacrifice of a teenager for power's sake,
They daily make.
However, they are paedophiles.
Possession is arresting the
Insight of this Spring to value a routine.
He is that man who has not felt
The world and can't say this gong
Of the Obsession
Is crueller than the spell,
That he calls the pretext
For reaching the end
Of his tether.
A blonde haired love,
Slowly fall, snow, because...
Because the soul of Galahad is for sale,
Now that he is briny and desperate like salt.
His infinite art is so proud it will destroy
His winded, windy legend and he sends
His heart as a present...
Slowly fall, my snow.

I want to have the peace of sloth.
You want to have realism,

And I'll give you the
Starched ventricles, which the force of gravity
Attracts, inciting my
Attack because, in my unconsciousness, I saw a truth,
In a red-blonde haired pale-faced girl,
Whose green eyes like feedback smile
And sanctify the blonde snow again.

The sea speaks,
"I can't translate its voice
Because there's a mystery
In these limbs.
Skinny assurances and a lost fay are in
My voice as bitter as bile.
If Inferno is white,
My very lamp flakes off.
You wouldn't dash out your thought
If it didn't throb because of the
Humour
Of the land
Which is like a sentence.
It won't be water
Which defuses the mines under the dunes,
But only another cloud
Which lost the pregnancy
Of the rain.
I'll find the Grail
To give back
What dispersed people beg for.
But if I may become a hero,
I'll tell you that
Apperception is the word
That can be
The cornerstone".

XIV. Hanged. A symbol

He loved the grass
Of the Vernal equinox when eclipses of
Sunlight burnt
The gas,
And maternal kisses of the earth
Revealed the adolescent features of Venus,
But the Christian God cut off the escape,
The illusions and the deluge, and the
Web of stars... So he feels the rivers
Of his veins bringing
Slow waves of blood. He is saying
"I am here now and it's devastating to lose
The Shape.
I was a stone, I lived through my Spring.
I listened to the voice
Which wells from the land
And exhales like clouds of air,
Waves of a heat that melts the ice and rocks.
Vitality whets appetite,
The will to survive.
"I want to have my future, I want to be more
Than a creature that consists of
Proteins and original comets..."
Magmas are so grand,
So various, so burning that he can't
Understand what they really mean and
Whether it is true or not that a word can quest for
The mystic tense,
Despite common sense.

He saw his friend, Will himself, hanged
By the neck and mute
His electric cells,
After a trial for witchcraft.
He guesses that it is cruel and desperate,

This flux, and the blood is only a memory of this
Swan, which killed itself.
"Why can't I finish my blown work
And have the last relief?
The limelight gave me a dig in the ribs
When what remains of me sat.
I am useless. I have felt only pain.
Please let me tell you the last world
I kept under wraps
The map of my body
Because I bodied forth Poetry itself
To make the Self bleed
And rebuild it".

XV. At home

It's Easter and he could live here
Where the grass is tender and the
Streets are fresh because of the rain...
So he can refuse his quest.
Yes, he will end up milking the audience
And fucking a pinup.
So, he'll have a tomb there, where his name
Will be written, because
His tracking down the sense
Was only a facet in the spectre of
The earth of the presences...
He has seen the face of a certain God
And the fragment of a sword.
He'll sleep dreaming of the day of
Those girls who took their own life.
Then, hazelnuts and mouths of roses...
They are like cosy ghosts...
I'd like to disappear.
This score which is my mind is hard
And when I stab my chest

I see a tremendous reaction from conscience.
Let time destroy the Self because
In this destruction, I could find a final port,
And there is pleasure in destroying oneself.
"Call me 'Legion'
Don't call me 'man'!"

"I hate and love birth as much as I hate fear.
You wanted a crystal? It's this book, it's here.
The stone which can scan your fear
And encompass the mystery
With this enclitic misery".

Everyman spoke, brushing his false teeth:
"There are times when
The Cosmos opens its petals
And lets its corolla shine.
At that moment I'd like to sleep
And dream of gleams
Which caress an immature dick
And the will. Then, the taste of day
Won't be full of regrets
And a parody of tragedy,
I live. I will die in my
Hollow sleep. Dances of women
Whose bodies remind you of an
Attempt to rise when you
Can hold the meaning
Of being here at hand, will
Be gentle and you'll be moved
By a bridge of wind,
Following the pace of rain.
Galahad will die with my old world
And my second skin
Will be rubbed off, leaving me
Free to say farewell to the
Clouds, to the Sun.

But, when other times demand
A different approach to life,
And you are given what
You have been looking for,
This means being at peace
With the pavement, and
The pebbles near the beach.
The impervious Bride screams.

My blood was an engine
And fuelled my movements
And spirited an infernal mood
In overwhelming my same
Mortal being. The world
Can't be forgiven and
A vestige of Europe is not
A proper aim, because the possession,
Which changes your voice, craves
Every land and I am possessed
By the bride, a hint
Which calls me to speak
And say how soiled was my vital
Lymph.
Wars
In one mind can't
Match the desire to lean over
And idle in the garden.
I know only that I am
Really pagan
And I want to pay nature, what's not mine.
But I love being here and mine
Is the power to annihilate every hope.
So my only hope
Is to see what I can't make out and
Then fuse this spell.
A man can't forget
He is a liar, but a talented one.

So I got addicted
And the secret is my sadism.
This was what I tried to hide.
However, I'll go to sleep
And dream of the battle between
The pollen and some thoughts,
The black birds I glanced at.

However, I will wake again
And bring the same war with me,
While going shopping, going to work.
I am not a fair creature.
I know that I am nothing,
A real biologist, but if I can become the guru
Of these gulls, I'll be happier
And become a vet and feel my same void
Fulfilled.
I understood that tasty is the infinite
But it's not for me,
Because I thrive, I rule the land,
And I have the power
To manipulate what's holy
And so I put it in a corner
Because the Saints consume your time.
I can't bribe them into
Accepting that this kingdom is mine
And so I am the butcher and the astronaut
Although there is a past
That is always there.

XVI. Self

"My weakness would like me to sleep.
But killing a mystery to find a Grail
Is a different attempt to fall".

"My mind was so full that it accepted as food
Only passion,
Because this beauty is crowned by these same lines.
However, the darkness is wet and the blood
Is good for painting. What then? I can say that
Everything came from the struggling of
A maid lying on the rocks and it's beautiful to kiss
Her veins, her skin,
Her glimmering skin deprives them of every detail.
Then, we opened our eyes again, and what
Pride wasn't able to inject,
Possession bought, and violated the bride,
The crystal of which her soul consisted
Gave in.
In the buildings along the river,
A glass of wine was thrown.
The wires of a new world
Promised it. So my possessed age is dying.
Man is not good and so he will find a god but
I can't renounce the reddest part of blood
Which was what I have been looking for.
And I want to die here
Singing the stanza about the war between
Dragon and man.
Chaos and me."

His quest alighted like a sparrow on his chest.
Because a noisy Grail is
His little Self, then silly arrangements
Become
A mixture of blood and nerves.
What is the origin of the wind? Plato's cave, maybe.
Small purple chops got rotten there,
He ripened among the roots
Of the European vocal chords.

"I wished I were the terminus.

A myth to another myth...
And I must admit
I'd like to quit.
This reflux of waters
Dispirits me and squeezes a tear.
It is true that in every myth
The hero must sleep amid
The Vernal limits and see
This lava.
The Self doesn't exist anymore.
The tragedy is to admit this.
This is the enigma of my laws".

And he was made to idle there
Where March rages and shrinks like
The sand that has been
Married to the chaste
Water of the rain.
The image of it is marred
By the excess of sense.
The Thames is beating
The pace of the dawn,
Perfect time for the enlightenment....
Your mind is not blank.
You want only to do
What is in yourself to do.
He will be where
The first presence was born,
The most ancient one,
The face of that same Self
Seduced
When this knight was young and
Yes, he yearned for the other part,
That particular path...
The sky
Was always there
Crowning the land,

Overhanging
Like the king which kidded
The same Galahad,
Who had sworn to go on
Against everybody,
Against everything
Only to state what
He was and was not
Because that voice
Ruffles a deep field

"Yes, I am... what I can see, what I understand.
That is the real matter with me, but Love is not hope,
The Light came from the outside, it has colours and forms
And I got insight into those moulds which are buried in me,
A cold cot of passions. You have shapes to think.
Will the last Roman shield defend Rome from the
Invisible barbarians who are
Like a tempest from North? Can a man build an empire?
The real heart brings life to the world, it's the concept
That's offended by a soul.
What was gentle....
There's a wall. You can't figure the veil
Put on the bird's bone to let you unveil the Fairy... "

"But I am a man, No!
And I put my hand on that same fire,
Because this limit offends.
I'll dispel the mystery
Which inflated me
Because if you spot your condition,
You'll die of Death,
A real book in the box.
I banned you men.
But a drive makes me think
We are prey of the same origins,
The difference is quality.

I am not better than you
Because my habit is resisting alone,
Against everybody. They are nonsense."

'You are an element, my lamb', Frances said.
"We'll be one but if you want to be naked.
Look to the sparrow and fall in a trance
To chase, to chase yourself.
Your memory is your Mother
But can the quest of the Grail undermine
Life and day? You'll fall
Like Spring leaves.
There will be the reckoning of the account
And the bill will be paid
In flashes
...Of fire. You can't know who you are."

XVII. Crazy heart

Shadows,
Waste paradises where the bones of
Angels lie,
Who fell during the battle of Amber
Against the forces of hell, in an array of what remains
Of the ideas I had about my land.
No, they are the bodies of other knights
Who failed questing for the Grail
And Galahad is anointed a Saint
Because he is the last of a bloodline.
Their armours reflect the light of the
Fall of sunlight!
The evening is eating his hands
And a cloak of prose destroys
Poetry decayed.
Pilgrims can sing their song about
A distant nation, when hunters of

Dreams slept...
He is so tired. "I beg the wind to make
My forces blow up in spirals of
Colours as bright as the souls
I had when I understood my naivety".
Galahad feels the mortal flavour of the excess and
He is so frisky that he would like to die
Prancing on his
Comprehension of the dark subject.
And so when the moon rises,
He tempts the universe into destroying
All these eyes, which in the stars we find
And to find out, in its flesh, a holy hush.
"My heart wants to love all this amount of life.
Unfortunately, a corpse is full of future life.
Everyman will inherit the land
This is the legacy of ecstasy.
When will I arise from my strident nature?
Why... Why do you forget
The individual culpability, the shrine
Of my Virginity?
Justice, Justice,
Where is my name?"

XVIII. South

He saw you, sinuous South,
Land of greasy corruption,
Loam of life and brain
Cancer...
And he took pleasure in
Being your light and becoming the
Angel of the Apocalypse.
So if he had been the law of God,
He would have damned his dog heart,
South, lost land,

The origin
Is a fairy in days of yore.
There is no salvation now,
Because he wants to live a tragedy
But, entrapped in a parody, doesn't pay
Attention to the fact that he
Offended the mystery.
There, it's flowering, the new eye
Beyond the prejudice, beyond the solstice
In a young woman, the sentence
Of a rebel Spring which hates
And demands
To eat all this chaos and work it out.

"I might have said that my pain
Is to last more than a moment,
But I didn't tolerate such a tangle
Of thoughts and Justice.
The Europe I dreamt about
Is the mortal daughter of
The Madonna of my Renaissance
Whose eyes are frescoed
And don't tell the truth
About the nature of my real Self
Which is more than the seductive
Knowledge I can have:
The soul as I saw it, alas,
When it was having bath
In a charming viscous sun.
I am besieged by Chaos.
The yellow murk in the swamp.
 A point in the sea. I lived too much".

XIX.   The price

"I know I am going to finish,
But surely not now, and I'll spare
This short amount of time to kiss
The ancient dragon
With my pain and spit my anger
As red as the blood
Of the Virgin of the rocks,
Because in this flesh was written
The fight and death of Galahad.
I was exiled and my eyes shake
Like the spirals drawn
By the flight of a fly
And you can say how deep the
Fascination of this limbo is,
Where there is no Moon
Because the lamps drug
This region of Inferno
Where I rule like a log in a pool...
Trying to cultivate potatoes in hell itself".

We are beings that simply "adjust"...
He hit the animal but he bleeds
And the veins of his hands blow up
Because of the winds,
Come out from the swamp.
The androgynous Dragon,
Comes full of suicidal will,
Scraping his face, he sees
The snakes chewing the throat of a hero,
In a vortex of dullness.
Chaos is killing
A certain lady Spring.
The origin, then the sin.
There's a voice Saint John described,
"At the eleventh hour"

The river will let
Its daughter knit this coat of
Maiden's hair.
Purity will last
The Empire won't fall.
"Mothers, you can have your cold sons back.
I, Galahad, who have seen the prospect
Of the Celtic seasons and have known
The girl and the snow, I will see
My body into a chasm
Of light and silk…
Fortunately, sinking in a drop of milk
As sweet as my
Poor meat".

Chaos is evil.
We are made to be only men.

XX.   A Regret

    Now, she is a constellation
        Among the firs that burn like candle,
        Draped by snow that cleans and melts to
        Penetrate the body - which howls.
  And her thought is another flash,
Because I dwelt where the shadows
        Melt away,
               And in a charming sigh of
                  Wind, the dream of fusing together with
Christ.

        I had a memory like a cloudy sky
But now her corpse is mine…
        The song, which Claire attunes passionately,
Speaks my Italian language:
            "Creation is nothing but

                    The first attempt...
Only Chaos lives and our life
            Is written in cold blood and water...
            Because you can't experience mere havoc,
The dissolution of your mind".
I have learnt this hard lesson
   Now, the truth is naked like
My decency that told me
            To forget she was a real woman...
                    But she was my wife,
The lost maid
         My real girlfriend and I have
                    Loved her since I was a child...
                        Struggling to have a creature of God
                        As a subtle bride.
                Our mind is a symmetrical
            System... It needs to be steady
And follow the logic to comply with its aim
            But the white lights keep on singing
                In a frosted accent:
  "The swan... Madonna's lily
   Became the swan..."

"I paid a high price
For my quest.
A body is a kind of map.
Frances,
With these lines I can't kiss your hair.
So I shaped you
To go beyond your fallen spirit
To refine our bodies
And swallowing my pride
My wife is still alive".

XXI. Frances

"She was my pagan goddess,
My Spring and my Saint Claire,
Because I know that the pity
Of her hand can't withstand the vernal
Smell of this daily citizen routine.
Her neck, a remembrance of
A swan, that forgives the branches
Arched over her hair ...
A neck of a naked swan
That remembers the
Chanson of a war between
Light and grey colours..
I smoked my mind, I sipped it
To absorb my modern essence
And blame again my carbon mixture.
And I drank the fog of her thought
And this smog poisoned
My lungs. I tried to identify with the chaos
But I gained insight into a truth which
Teaches how to despair,
How to cry your eyes out,
To symbolize
What chaos is. Desperation, I mean".

She, my shocked fairy appears,
Fat seas against well-cleaned cliffs,
The sky became gory to be seen and her
Blonde free hair was a red flaxen ensign
In those clouds...
She shatters my will
And instils a sneaky voice in my will which shrills,

"Another time, a life for only a pregnant
Action and so your mind will be mine"...

In a church her effigy,
The silent saint of crying...
She didn't know: what is the light
But the gloomy side of my eclipse?
Her cheek flushed but that red
Reminded everyone only of old penitence.
She was young, once, and her heart throbbed
Because of thoughts too sharp.
But her body was always perfect of that perfection
That only blood deserves.
Then she was welcome into the skies
But truth was dead
And she with it.
A monk said, bringing tragedy to the scenery:
"Frances is with us no more".

Frances, a shred of my mother's white dress...
Painted in her flesh by the ventricular blood of her heart,
And by the final sentence of rest

XXII. Vexillum

i

I can't deny being possessed
By an angel.
I dreamt of killing Every-Man to say
"I am more powerful than Time,
And this life does not deserve
To be tasted by lust".
When you sink in your mood,
You'll sing the anger which destroyed
My mouth because
"If Everyman wins,
I will be doomed to be a fossilised tree".

ii

Two opposite beams...
Then I who was borne
Where Lament rends
Its tears
Between this being and this non-being,
The infernal choice...
Can Spring rise to Heaven?
I dwell there
And cry for the whim
Which has led me to the land
Not blessed by the sun.
A new twilight surfaces
And the icicles of chaos
Are just at hand.
I had
A soul which still lasts.
An outcast
Has to face the eternal
Moment of the fairy.

I am the way, so, I can accept
"Nothing" and rest...
The gleam of the first body
Is without the silver gown.
She was that memory
Which had conceived the shapes.
What about me?
I am only the spit of my swan.

There's a room in which old people moan
And talk about the story of a swamp.
It was built with a cross which had
To close the door which ushers man to Hell.
It's said that now they smeared it with carbon and steel...
But they don't think

That the crosses are made
To horrify and
Turn up when the civilisation is not civil
And politeness takes over sacrifice.
A mile from it you can see that sea
And understand the fictive nature
Of this slush because we advance,
Losing the scale, which kept us grand.
The problem is that you have not only
A carnal being
And this is what I feel in the guts.
You are horny while you feel!
And then you hate what disturbs your
Bland conception of yourself,
But your mind can be grand
And perceive the nakedness of what you lost,
I mean Time itself, the mime of every ghost.
Better never to have been born.
The rest is a compromise.
I happen. Hence I am.

XXIII. Mediterranean Sea

"And so after this quest,
I am here, my sea, and I see
That child who would
Take away this wind with a little
Shell, and so, my Catholic, European sea,
I, who died,
I am here to kiss this chaotic age
And to cry all my tears because
I sold the Grail, I'd like to lose my Self
In the dissolution of love
Without any form of sense...
Rivers come back and the seasons
Play with the wind, buried cities sleep

Under the waves of rhythmic prose
Because mud and mad love were fused
In my blood and my nature feels
The end of this prospective spring...
Heroes
Are here, in a tomb of sand and sadness
Where weakness will not sing...
I came from Nowhere
And losing my language, I kept track of
The legions of waves...
My sprayed feelings...
There isn't a plot, but I am here, my
Mediterranean sea, and this water's sin
Would be saved now, when the sunrise
Kisses the fog and an embryo
Becomes a man and a promise...

Now, after my death, I am here.
I'll let my heart sleep here
Where the breath of the Sun changes a mind
Into a saintly bride of dusts and sea pride... Now,
I am only feeling your fingers.
Now, I will be Galahad.
Only now I am seeing the Grail,
Heaven which lets you win against
The evil and
Hug that same Cross, rebirth
Over pride, something more than chalk.
But now the chalice
Doesn't inspire me, I must drink
I can take on my human features
I can take them over
But is the Grail only the truth?
I see only my Frances, maybe
My mother who was a Jewish girl.
I kneel. I am won,
Modernity failed.

Everyone can laugh.
I accepted that time
Can't be stopped,
The Julian calendar
Ran with the tide.
There was in me
The love for a girl
Which is natural
And in Latin
Is called "speranza, hope".
I am ready to follow my girl.
I want to die, accepting the dying hues of Death."

XXIV. Solitudinem faciunt...

Melted are the shapes of wax,
The revelation is clear
And has the flavour of salt,
Because if you stare at her,
Into her still face,
You will be turned into this dull salt.
Hypocrisy helps to survey,
Maybe to survive.
A thought of good and evil
Can hurt your upset guts,
Maybe it can really gut.
The shapes
Which the Self is built on
Catch fire and shine
Like the iris
Of an obsessed eye. Ancient idols,
Worn out, fall.
They are the army that swarm
Like a cloud in our land and storm
What decency was about.
We are left with an idea.

To survive and crave the existence of the plants
Because we are rooted in the ground like them
And we are useless like a psalm.
The fault was to be
What we simply are, beings that build prejudices
About the mild existence we were gifted with.
Ho, everything implodes and
Then, there is the rest,
Which can't be mine, because of the quest.
I can't have wanted it
Because I imagined that a blonde presence
Had breastfed me,
Pacing a rhythm, hinting at a kind of pledge.
But you will have your genuflections.
Walking tomorrow to buy bread and milk...
Only to wean the soul from tilting at celestial things!
You will sweep into this flavourless air.
This life is so inflated
That its wave rises and squashes.
The conscience sloshes...
Everything seems to be calm ash
And the snow belongs to the Past,
Because, actually, it snows volcanic chalk.
But in this fading away of the future
Galahad embraces his last symbol,
The first sparkle,
And tearing off
An atom from the sky,
From its sprayed body,
He brings with him the cross of his mother
And falls where there is no darkness
And I become one with the little lamps,
Silly and fused with this darkness,
Unconscious, oozy light,
The nest of sunset.

XXV. The backfire of being the just fourth horseman - Confession

i

The sap is dense and spills slowly by.
This is the drama of a knight,
Because beyond justice there is space
And you can't burn the landfill
Of my fickle way of feeling the world
Which unnerves me...
A feeling of pity makes you run
To where you were born.
They scoured my will,
So I am featureless like a saint.
I lost my flesh and its thrilled when
They rammed into me the belief that I was useless,
Because far from imagery sprouts concrete.
The hues of the world have an end,
The rent is this white shroud, a sickness
Called sympathy for the doomed.
The wing of my second birth
Destroyed the apparition.
A man who writes
About a new truth, needs it. I mean the blood.
Why can't I be like you
And graze as you, cattle, used to do?
My Frances was a whim.

I am a maddened judge
Making a lure of desire out of her hair.
She's the heir of Spring,
The skinny girl, the witch, "Frances,
the sparrow, the Spring"
The first mother sings.
"Where is the sin?"
I am mindful of my memory.

I did have the choice to deny my storm of words.
To recount a story in a plot, is
To slay the dragon!
The dragon, a man.
I wound up being old.
What was rinsed,
Is buried in what was a slim chest.
The rivers feed into the sea,
The gleam of a brackish god.
However, this piece of sky
Floats over an eternal cry which reminds me of
The fact I am Galahad. I hand over this heart.
I want to be eaten to grow out of you.
The swan, my last clue.

ii

The centre has got to be the limit,
There is a time when purity
Can transfix your heart and the demons
Remind you of something which was lost:
This is pain.
I was challenging my God.
I can't understand the sense of the mighty.
This is a hard rhythm because
The shadows are unbearable for me
And I decry in other men cries of help,
The same as mine

And worst of all is to discover you don't have wings.
So, this is what I discovered on Silbury Hill and
I wanted to push off to break every fence and hence
To break even with my past, but this lasts:
"The world is stronger than me".
Take your last hope.
I, Galahad, am in front of this wall of fire.

The path shivers
If a daughter of Eve created me another will be the vertex
Of the will. Maybe I confused Will with Dick,
But in the sea I saw the mirage of
Vision every age must find..
My mother is fading in the moor where lines
Turn the abstract into a human face
And it finds a pause...
Heaven is like a game.
God is your limit
And provokes you.
In his mind you are a joke
I can't trespass the boundary.
My epic bears the brunt.

XXVI. De Profundis. Itinerarium Mentis in Deum

i

My very flame makes me the dragon
And I can't expect the tongues will spare me.
I am worse than you.
I am a priest that peeps to have a look
At the lasciviousness Modernity might be.
It is a sad legend and now
It is high time I wrote my de Profundis,
To found the legend of the limit.
Why was the core so shining as
To be unbearable for my queen?
This is not my world.
The atom has its wreath
The score is Mozart's Requiem and I want to sing along
With the echo of a future,
Far from me, structures maybe.
Because this occasion requires strength
I don't pretend to have and
The weakness drugs

My lungs and the breath,
Now I fancy the Requiem, the rest.
The heart is only another weight
I would get rid of.
In this body there was a map.
I wish I had died before the apprehension
That I was fated
Like the bullets which
Cannot hit the pope's ribs.
Why can't I be a different knight?
So Galahad is another mask
Of Romanticism
Which has to sink to where
The night jumps out of the earth.
I tend to recollect images
Of the arts but what is 'explosion of sin'?
The past... another myth
If Heaven falls to me, how can I fall to Heaven?
I last. This is the guilt:
"The world is stronger than me"
The poetry of God spits blood.

ii

The secret is Time, its old pot
In which fear grins.
If you open the floodgates, they can't be closed again.
This is the last quip.
If you burn like beryl, you can't swallow the halo.
So my nature loved itself and now, it is pale.
Along the river I pour the secret of the Fall.
Mermaids, blonde Christian meaning,
Symbols of something lost, hello!
Everything, my heart,
Will remain the same, recalling its origins in the sea.
The voice will beguile the mirror and
Will keep on being

As beautiful as the ring
My Fairy refused.
The traces and the stains
Won't melt the mist
Because I accept the body of a vision
That ends up being
The parching obsession of my queen.
Everything for the bridal veil.
The mind, the ancestral hag,
Despite the plinth
On which it sits can't reign
Over the hills.
To put forward a new world
Is an action for a saint.
I hovered in my dark side.
The ancestors had their part.
Beyond any friendship.

iii

I belong to the Past
And this arm is the heir
Of an aristocratic bloodline
Which judged what's real,
What good and what harmful.
And so I floated on a world
Where Beauty was only one.
The pious won't get away with murder.
Maybe...

iv

The green Heaven gives no relief.
I said:
"Do you want to be a demigod?"...
Here, immortality is close.
These currents are eddying and maybe err...

My mind again?
But this level is beyond me.
He who has been touched, can only yearn again...
To complete the yarn and be wise?
But the star has stolen the effect.
I can imagine what happens but cannot see...
So my strength strands...
I understood that the rain has a rhythm.
The song sucked me dry.
Here, is this the Grail?
I am not a part of you.
The jingle sings:
"You are beyond..."

v

And so the sunrise will kiss the dawn
In the erotic hug of West and East in the breath
Of the Earth,
It will be like a blanket of snow and
Of weed, and jellyfishes will enliven
The wedding
Of what's abstract and the real world, because
Symbols are clear here
Leaving the backwash washing
The front of the Angel and licking like a dog what I was
As if the tender waves
Were kisses for
One who wants to come back
To the concave breast. I
Saw the Grace,
That one taming the Angel of Apocalypse
With a hiss.
The Miss came from the Lake
And there I found a cove,
The water was not peaty but calm
The implosion of my nerves passes by where

The mirroring lights
Pollen on the face of the sea
Completely new.
The rest is my reward...
A new peak crops out, the peak, the height of my desires,
Pointing to the skies like a spear...
I can't come back to this tongue of land...
The horizon I melted in.
It's easy to bless what's beyond you.
And so I hunted for God
But now I see that there's no path
Apart from oblivion,
Which can't touch the first, the real core. And so
I feel another hand, Madonna's hand,
Gently touching my hair
And dragging me away.
I want to hold God back.
He said he is still a man,
He is the truth, He,
The Word.
Man inherited the land.
The rock is fissile like shale.
He built on it.
Dirt and Chaos darken the Sun...
What happened to the law?
Then, he politely asked,
"Do you love me?".
I am full of sensations, won and pure.
Love is heat, it's the meaning of the spring
Which permeates Heaven and its bliss.
So I got fused to Life.
I saw God
In my resistance
I see the surface of the sea,
Those streaks that are liquid shades from between.
From the bottom where the Sleeping Beauty,
Consciousness lies,

Human features, a cry, then
A red cell, surrounded by a whirl;
I was the Sleeping Beauty
And seeing the world born from God's fire
Is like being under the water
And seeing how the currents move the sea.
I was the Sleeping Beauty
And seeing the world from God's eye brought
Perfection of peace which encompasses me
And that hot air combs me while
Everything is present and detailed.
I was in the heart of God.
Wind and fire, interwoven,
Threaded spectacularly still
In a drop of blood
Which attracted like the force
That awakens the day.
I saw the failure of Modernity
But we can't have
A past.
His word breathed love into me.
Now I am above the flux of misery
Which demands "Justice must be done
If Life is a gift, you must give it".
Now, He floats over me.

His word is not bleak.
I'll be that blond boy who
Had curls like tears.
I am at last.

vi

Then, when the Western wind
Brought chaos where the doom was born,
Frances unveiled the shoulder
That coincides with that white flower,

The fairy which cries the dawn of another world,
Of another life,
Virgil's Virginity,
The shot of light...
She is a ray
I was astray
Like that dart which to the Sun speaks plainly:
"Have a daughter, praise the flower and preach
Each of you will face the limit which
As humble as a mane
Of chestnut hair
Was before.
Heaven won't be tasted.
You will become an Angel with no sex.
Galahad is there in the vanishing point
As vain as another law:
Nature will be that drop
Of blood trickling on the cloth
Which is now hot because
It was the veil Frances gave
To the mind.
You'll go to
Trespass on death's realm
To be with her without revenge.
What has split him,
Now will be blessed.

A couple will be a constellation
As in the past.
Three words, the chest of the swan.
The identification with the storm.
My God, I'll close the door of chaos so as to be a token
Of human nature.
I emptied my Soul.
I renounced my power,
I must find the sense
Of my soul

And Frances is light
But what's been gained, must be cared for
Must be shared.

XXVII. The young mestiza, the daughter

The young mestiza turns up among the confusion
Of my mind, among buried fragments of a world.
The brown curly hair which reminds you
Of the beginning of Spring when the time of light drags by,
But lets you understand that pregnant is the earth
And miracles of Madonna's lily,
The flower of Christ, are going to bloom.
The mestiza caresses your tender side, your feminine
                                                    insight...
And then her iris is green, a green so bright
It makes you feel the borders of the sky.

The clouds, the grey rag
Of an immature day can go by,
I feel the nakedness of my mind
Which understands
That purity can't be dull,
Because this chaos is won
And the virginal way
Of thinking whispers to your soul
That the sun belongs
To Light and Light has a weight,
Is full of carnal tones
Which emerged from muscles
And fire. I was the angel
Of the Apocalypse and I dreamt
Of destroying history
To be able to speak again
About the perfection
Of essence but I confused

The brightest part
With the tangy smell which
Surrounds a simple mind
And drives you to drink:
And so my mind realised
That Beauty is different,
Is beyond the line, in the wind,
Beyond what you used to think.

The daughter, pleased by her own neck,
Wore a cloth of fresh sap,
Increasing the power of the eye,
Sympathising
With the pain which is hidden from the magnetic
Contraction of stars, I feel, I have a name
However, I was born to do, to act.

I'll destroy my past, I'll cradle the second birth
I'll destroy the mirror of time,
Because
Silver is cold when it's not married
With the sliminess of blood.
The knight will come again, will be stronger than
Every havoc which waits for every man
And his colour of
An ancestral fault... but now this has
A new voice, because the purity is not as
Simple as I thought. The wedding of two different seas
And the birth of this girl whose shadow is not dark,
Remind you of piles of brown earth.
I would shape my heart.
A girl's body reveals that you want to be
Always young with blood which runs into
My last premonition.

I confessed my future. I eradicated my past.
Beauty is not a blonde, it has a new taste.

The White sucked the blood and was drunk...
Madonna's lily, the abstract chant
Are one with
The carnation of the heiress of the land.
I use my name which is Domenico
And now I'll show you how naked I am.
You can't understand that I was mild
And followed the movement of the wind,
But then the fire sparkled
And pain encircled me.
I was saved by an idea. I am not like you.
Now, this contradiction dictates to my
Character and activates it.
I want to percolate in you
Like a shower of meek brown rain that
Inspires the steam of youth,
The mood of the South
I never had. I always behaved like a man,
Brought up to bear sorrow
And live for a dream,
Be forever young and be in love
With the soul of the creatures encircling me,
Singing about the battle of a man and a beast.
My fury is in the pit.
I am younger than I should be
Because the wounds are the story,
But we can go into the river
And have our moult.
We'll come out different.
I'll be your ghost.
I'll touch the souls of your daughters and sons.
What I lost must be yours.
This is the kiss I want to impress on Frances' lips.

The body of Galahad was given to the moody land
That withstands words of pity and shame because his
                                                    name

Is written in the mane of grass, as green as his past
And mean misery is the mystery of sand and seed
Of which everyone consists, cyst of mist...
Fallen deep in lukewarm wind that carries swarms
Of flowers as white as the verse of his voice.
He had no choice and let his hand, poised between
                                    two worlds,
Caress the tresses of the maid, Frances that is.
Sometimes
She is hope, sometimes death.
A drama
Of space and time appears. He had to cope
With fires that ravaged his equivocal age.
A war is wagged when a baby is born.
The corn accepts the rain. Water cannot wash pain
And his smile is and is not a stain.
Time goes on under Sun and Moon.
Maybe this son simply swooned.

www.ingramcontent.com/pod-product-compliance
Lightning Source LLC
Chambersburg PA
CBHW021120080526
44587CB00010B/583